# A packet of seeds

by

Bernard M Coldwell

Aquabatiques (two blokes called me)

ISBN 97890821267



Aquabatiques is a term and project used for the creative ideas that flow like constant streams of water.
Sometimes they are heavy and sometimes they are still but they are always present.

Aquamatiques is a term and project used for the creative sounds that flow like water.

Both terms Aquabatiques and Aquamatiques are of my own creation and therefore do not exist in a dictionary.

A Packet of Seeds is the title of this booklet.

# A packet of seeds

**Foreword**

Being one of little words I cannot think at this moment in time of what is what was and what will be. At this very moment as I type this there is outside in the street below an environmental truck making one heck of a noise whilst stinking the beejezus out of everything and am sitting here trying to keep me head screwed on. I cannot think straight what with the thought the street must be full of over flowing toilets or something that is really the pits. Blocking nostrils with a cloths peg ain't gonna help much.

A little bit about me is that I have been writing poetry and prose since my teenage years and have spawned some creative ideas in that time and it is here that I hope to share some of these with you.

My personal life is not one that I like to talk about at ease with strangers as I find it a tough enough subject and on the whole is way too complicated anyway. What I can say is this; I was born in England, raised in Wales and live and reside in Belgium. I am bi-lingual English and Dutch.

My likes are listening to good music viewing the classic movies and lots of reading. I am passionate about ancient worlds their civilization, artifacts in a wide variety of archeological finds from all over the world. I am also interested in UFO's and time-travel the use of technology though more on that at a later stage.

**Publications** have been in the form of group efforts anthologies some can be found on various websites across the internet.
God Bless You was published by Watermark Press in An Hour at Sunrise.
Believing is the Answer by Watermark Press in Flowering Splendor
Unique by Nobel House in Theatre of the Mind
Perhaps You'll Understand by Watermark Press in The Language of Memory
Coffee Pause by Watermark Press in Best of Poems and Poets
The Sunflowers by Watermark Press Who's Who in Poetry
Chimney Stacks(part one) by Nobel House in Centers of Expression

This book contains pieces that have been written over a period and it is my sole and personal effort to writing a book of my own.

At present time I am an active member and moderator for the writers' group The Surreal Circus offered under the Gather umbrella and consequently have had several poems published through them. The most recent of which is in the form of two anthology books entitled Twisted Shorties I and II. You can find more on that by visiting Gather.Com for more detail of the on-going project.

Please note that this work or solo project is not a book of a journalists dream nor is it meant to be comprehensively or grammatically correct – though it is sometimes more of a comical point of view into a journey of self-discovery ideally a book to always return to for when inspiration is needed.

Other projects to date are:

Aquamatiques these are self-made compositions of electronic experimental dreamscapes and are meant purely as experimental.
Inca's as Stinkers was also a dreamscape recording using minimal electronic instrumentation.

If you want to get in touch you can find me at http://about.me/bernardmcoldwell or on Twitter @coldwellbm

**Acknowledgements:**

Many thanks go to the many family members that are both far and wide, my friends(they know who they are, home and abroad), my ex-workmates, ex-colleagues and to all my acquaintances that over the years have met me and put up with my weird sense of humour and some very awkward moments. I thank you for being you.

**Packet of Seeds:**

## Oyster!

On the fourth of July she was packing
A peck on the cheek for her time
Says; "Never spend nothing'
Give it all away
To a charity somewhere out there today"

Oh, I never knew how easy it was
To get lost on a memory so good
Both feet on the ground
Needed to know
What was it that really mattered most?

I am touched by the smile that you gave me
Taunted by release in the wild
Then I could never come close to this
A day to go on with nothing on the coast

You planted those seeds deep within me
I locked it in only back then
As I look at you now
My heart not good enough somehow
It hurts me inside and displeases

## Affairs of the heart

Affairs of the heart always make me cry
I try to live and I almost die
Those strange, strange people
And their unique ways
Portray a life
That's so unreal

Some beg, some borrow
Some move along
Some steel
Some try to make a deal

But most of all
I find
I try
To keep my friends
Separating wheat from rye

Temptations come - temptations leave
The points of view
All written in the eyes
And I love you's!

## Perhaps you'll understand

I have always told the truth to you
I can never tell a lie
For there's something about you lady
A THING that catches my eye

No I cannot write it down on paper
A feeling I once felt
It's harder now than ever
To tell you how I felt

Your smile it brings me hunger
Unlike some other wolf
A feeling of desire
Of home just like it should

I know that you don't know me
I only wish you could
For we live a different life now
Both of us understood

God create-th man
To figure out his plan
But if I know you so well
Perhaps you'll understand!

## Sunday Musings

Lewd, crude and never prude?
Cooed, mooed and never sued?
Abused, accused and somewhat dejected.
Billified, petrified, hung drawn and quartered!
Old testament that is detriment
Pre-sequal to an all
Let's congregate
Let's judicate
The blackards got a case of old rum
Ol' pirate?
"Ye me hearties; stealin' robbin' lupins, codgin's what say ye now to old dodgin's?
Oo aargh me hearties, oo aargh!
Well, shiver me timbers I got struck by woodworm me Lord
Looks like I got no leg to stand on no more
Best start that old fire up and you can kiss these meatballs right on outa 'ere, aye!"
Judge Turmoil states quite loudly;
"Hang him by the legs til warm!
May the flames of life ever ignite you..
May God rest his sock!"

## Coffee Pause

He don't like the coffee
He don't like the tea
He just wanna get on
and do as he please

Water unjust bitter taste in his mouth
Leaves a hole in his pocket
When he wanna fly south

He's very ambitious
He knows quite a lot
Knows of the dangers
But speaks of them not

He tries to remember
a time he once had
In a room full of fools
And a life he ain't got

Sometimes he's cool
Sometimes he not
'cuz he's got the experience
Somethings we've not!

## Believing is the answer

I was no good then as I am no good now
Refuge has gotten to me I don't feel proud.
Some people make mistakes
I can see it anyway
But helping me develop
My senses are away

Believing is the answer
It's the only way
Until that day you realize
It's a role in life you play

So forget all your anger
Dry up all those tears
Just stand back for a moment
Nurture all your fears

You don't need an answer
It's as plain as you can see
Further more the questions
It's not what it may seem

Love is what you needed
Bare to every bone
Skinned under your nose though
You press and press alone

Why don't you answer questions?
That love hath donned you so?

## Sunday Musings as a kid

As a kid;
One fine day I'm gonna lay in the hay and watch a movie with Molly Ringwald.
One fine day I'm gonna get to see the Hopscotch and Claire 'd Lune.
From Waltham City and those Buckeroo's
Chinese lanterns with some Shanghai noodles
Go deepsea diving, or go way out west
Then come back here cuz its the best.
Eat cold bacon butties, or hang about in me see thru vest.
On one fine day am gonna get by
That's one fine day one day at a time

## Insomniac

Mild, wild insomniac
Dreams of a lover on her back
Legs wide open, spread apart
Makes love like a maniac.

Frizzle, frazzle fumble free
Putting on a mask
That's plain to see!

Dizzle, dazzle troubled me
What an empty place
This turned out to be.

All alone along the wire
We all hear - we all retire
Somehow mate - you missed out
Sorry for the mess and all that shower!

Someone's got to pay but it's not me
You upset the applecart
Count your blessings be.

Once you were a stranger
Climbing up a tree
Looking out for dangers
You don't see me!

Death has got an answer
Don't know what it is
Couldn't speak the lingo
Guess no-one ever did!

## Love Is...

Love is.. looking when she notices
A stare in her eyes - rise up
Like a moonlit night
Feelings of emotion
That lasts and lasts and lasts

Face is.. colour turned on for me
I'm all hot and bothered
Sometimes this means stop to me
Yet sometimes I am not bothered

In love there are no disguises, no reprises
Feelings of maturity
You weave and flutter all around
Eyes that shine light up the sky
It's here that heaven's abound

Three feet high I wondered
With a smile
Both feet on the ground
'cos love was all around

When she got into hip hop
I was into folk
Her head so sore of sorrow
I was full of jokes

When I am lonely
I wander about then I cried
Those things are getting to me
I feel I wanna die
Then some angel comes to me
She says: 'you are your own'
Why don't you love her like a lady
And not like the telephone!

## Bicarbonate

Bicarbonate of soda
Those things that make you older
Well I know now that that isn't true

Saint-Stephen went a-bruising
He couldn't stop abusing
Well I know now that that isn't true

Circumference the goldfish
Two castles, that is so rich!
Cor blimey, that that it isn't true!

Oh lordy, lordy lordy
Esquires much the poor meat
Oh I know now that that isn't true!

Christmas cards the times is hard
For those that ain't got plenty
Though I know now that that isn't true!

A New Years Day we gotta sway
An' kiss ol' Aunties whimpers
Yeah, I know now that that isn't true

Easter eggs your ghosts are dead
A chicken there more likely
A rabbits foot on Colby's hook
We're getting there more lately
But I know now, that that isn't true!
Well I know now, that that isn't true!

## Two bit hooker

There's a two bit hooker on a number nine bus
It don't mean much when you do it in the rough

Up or down the alleyways nothing's turned away
'cos you get cold feet when your Willie's in pain

Don't be getting clever - your heart it ain't that soft
Don't be very different - your heart it ain't that soft
Don't try hard to deny it - you're the funny sort by half

Undertakin' legals, well ain't that the bitch that do
Fiddlin' here the business? Well, nothing doing to

Don't be getting clever - your heart it ain't that strong
Don't get all excited - your heart is ain't that soft
Don't try hard deny it - you're the funny sort by half
No use try to beat it - that's just the way it is!

## Kookaburra

I was standing on the corner of the street
When a little old lady said to me
She said; do you have a kookaburra stuffed up your jumper?
Upyerjumper? Upyerjumper?
And I said; "No!, no! no! no, no."

She said; "Now, don't get telling me all those lies
I can see it, I can see it in your eyes.
That kookaburra, kookaburra near your thighs
Is taking me, it taking by surprise!"

And I said; "Lady, with all the haze I can endure
You are the one that's gone for sure
Coz I ain't got a kookaburra up my jumper
Up my jumper
It's a loin thing,
A loin thing!"

## Sunday Musings In a court of honor

In a court of honor
Harriet Harper of 52 Crescent Drive is accused of witchcraft and vampirism.
"Ms Harper how do you bleed, the guilty or the non-guilty?" asked the lawyer.

"Non-guilty your honor - all that lovely whiteness it's like a dream!!
Ooh the guilty ones - well they are a nightmare. Before you can get one of those you have to either be stoned or have tomatoes thrown in your face. You never know with them...and I can tell you too. This isn't Walford you know. There, at least you got a bath before any given stoning. Ooh the rituals some people keep nowadays its enough to bleed yer heart out.
Ooh, of which I don't have your honor - I'm heartless, cruel, very cruel, selfish, unkind and also very, very mean."

"Yes, yes Ms Harper - just answer the question with yes or no!"

## Fifteen Jokes

Fifteen jokes on a number nine bus
One good chap taken outa the back
Unto known brothers changing attire
Felt like something's gotta give

Ha ha ha ha ha did he ever admit
Down on the tarmac giving it stick

Suddenly the blue light
Fighting for the might
Running up an acre
Fold it ever tight!

Currently a siding
Back to untold walls
You don't get any fun
Sittin' out there in the hall

Call me cozy, call me great
Call me anything, you relate!
Call me crazy, call me nuts
Call me a cab, its all too late!

## Spooks?

What will you do when the spook gets you
Will you run - will you hide
Or will you bottle it up inside?

Remember there's a saying:
Most end up by praying.
When you gotta go you gotta go
Never mind the bother, the hassles or the tossers
Just pick up your senses and then you walla!

Now when evening comes around
You can hear it in the sounds
Of good old Mother Nature
Giving it to you

You need not be offended
Held up or apprehended
Just pick up your senses and relent it!

If and when the time comes
You'll remember when your mind hums
Don't forget your ego; it's a drag!

It's but a minutes worth
Pray to God and all his good
Offer help unto your friends
Because they help you in the end
Just pick up your senses and depend!

As for all the pools of water
Music's so sweet as that of Porters
You'll find that little comfort in a home
Be it up or be it down, yet never with a frown
Keep on smiling in the end
Then pick up all your senses and defend!

## Ho Chi Min

Who stuck the boot in Ho-Chi-Min?
Giving him what for - stickin' it in!
I got a can out, blue and round
Contents no good, deafening sound
Now, I wanna know who kicked my friend
He's gonna cop it in the end.

Sales up the jumbo - knockin' 'em down
Really the mongers - croppin' it now
Same ol' peculiars selling my gaf
To all the angels at our café

Now, I wanna know who's puttin' it in
Gathering data - kickin' my bin
I wanna know who stickin' it in
Pullin' the flags down - burning my sticks
Daft ol' petunia's - flakin' it thin

So who put the boot in Ho-Chi-Min
Stitched up a tiger - wearin' it thin
To all the angels - makin' me sick
Makin' me nervous - takin' the piss
Drawn in the nonsense - pullin' my stick

Is this a record - you are wearin' me thin
I wanna know who stickin' it in!
I'll tell you something - it ain't right
Learned it at high-school - late at night
Fall is the graceful - he's not doin' it right

So, who put the boot in Ho-Chi-Min
He's making me nervous - wearin' me thin
Giving him what for - makin' a din
I wanna know who's kickin' it in
Who's making me nervous, wearin' me thin

I wanna know - 'cos it's not me
Dressing me perfect though I can't see.

## Somewhere in the green isles of home called Ireland. Stately.

"Did you hear about that cleaning lady called Mrs. Teesdale, Eamon?" enquires Mrs. Peabody.

"She was the runner of a brothel you know. Oh, and did you hear about how she got her son Dougle now?

Apparently she'd been seeing this boy at work and she told him that they had lot of sex where she lived and thrived upon it".

Seamus; who in his curiosity, went over there to the stately looking home of an evening just for a little peep. He was looking through one of the curtains from inside the front lawn trying to see what the Teesdales actually got up to.

What with him standing there, clutching his torch in the dark and all. He must have been there all about three and a half minutes when old mother Teesdale had spotted him and invited him in for some tea and biscuits. Of course, being ever so shy, Seamus apologized and went inside then sat down in the parlor whilst old mum Teesdale went off to fix a pot-o-tea.

Meanwhile the young Teesdale came in, sporting a whole new looking vacuum cleaner. She must have got it from Havards on one of her many visits to the Yorkshire Dales though am not quite sure. "Seamus, what are you doing here at such an hour?" she asks, "why I haven't finished gathering up all the fluff from the last lot and there's a already a new visitor; I'll be with you in a minute" she went on.

Seamus, at this time, was struck with fright. His knees tightly clutched together creating a bulge near his underpants. Then suddenly out of the blue, Ma Teesdale arrives with tea on a tray with some cracking shorts on, wearing only a smile and some do-yer-lipstick.

Seamus quickly took hold of the tea bags and started to dunk them into the hot water. His bulge, by now, was getting a lot bigger. Ma Teesdale asked if he would like a bit of crumpet. Whereby Seamus had lost all sense of control and whipped out the flashlight that was protruding in his underpants.

## Drawn and Quartered

Well I remember back in fifty-nine
The sweet tall stories and one hell of a time
One-eight of Feb something started in me
It was 2am when all the trouble broke free
A tight fisted rover put on his white shoes
Took off into the night to dance away his blues
Not a smile! Not a photograph! No sign of life!
Gone was the great one and gone was his wife
Off with another one deep into the night
No family! No disrespect! No alimony! No guarantees! No future! No we haven't met yet!

Well we all got back about 63
Where my daddy wanted you more than he ever wanted me
Broke down slow - throw down the rope hold
As the earthquake was coming but I couldn't get a hold
The hospital nurse said you're a lucky little man
To fall down the staircase I'll fix the best I can
I was the aquarian sun! He was the American sun!
An' he was and he was and he did and I didn't
He was he and he was and he did and I didn't

Those cheap little lies borne into the sky!
When it's calm I think of these
The troubled times and their trickeries
My brothers laughed while I scorned a lot
Believed in my blood yet my dreams are all to cop
I'm mesmerized now by the sound of a boy
Who's into rock and roll and his great big toys
Like to think I'll join him but I don't see how
'Cos somethings coming on and I just don't just don't know!

Blessed rainbows! Forever chasing blessed rainbows
One's coloured blue and the other one is yellow
Some of it is cool yet some of it is valor
Put it on hold babe, put it on hold
We'll save it for later..'cos somethings coming on and it feels a lot safer...
And now there's just some letters
From mother one or two
Explains of the dangers
But who cares, when it's over!

Life is no taboo! No No taboo
Life, life is no taboo, no no taboo
When your in trouble..deep deep trouble.

## From Today And Tomorrow

Here I stand
Holding my head up high
I'm looking to see
What's beyond the sky
All I see are broken angels
I'm looking to see
Will that happen to me?

'cos down here on the ground
There's a crisis going on
They're killing me first
Before the battles begun
I fear there's no evil
They're taking my blood
They're spilling it everywhere
Til justice is done
My friends they will follow
From today and tomorrow

Here I stand
Holding my head up high
I'm looking to see
What's beyond the sky
I guess I am facing
My death is at hand
The life I once had
Has gone to the land

'cos down here on the ground
There's a crisis going on
I guess they'll forgive me
When the battles has won
I won't fear no evil
I won't feel no pain
'cos I won't be here
To see it again!

'cos down here on the ground
There's a crisis going on
They're killing me first
Before the battles begun
I fear, there's no evil
I won't feel the pain
Sold off to the young ones
Sold off on the game!

## Green By Years

In a town where everybody's happy
In a town where everybody's clean
You watch this industry grow by night
And fall by breach of peace

Well your mother never gave you nothing
Not a bit of solid gold street
We all found out about your Mother
She was delicate and none too sweet!

So you can put up your umbrella
Put on your blues suede shoes
Don't call me: 'I'm the innocent one'
You're no fool but some kind of fella
Yeah, you're no fool but some kind of fella

You are green by years
Have nothing to fear
Yet your attitude is none too clear
Why not get yourself back on the streets?

So, put down your umbrella
Forget the evening speech
Don't call me: 'I'm the innocent one'
You're no fool but some kind of fella
(we all get toiled and tethered)
(we all get toiled together)
(we're all just toys to weather)
(we're all just ploys together)
But you are some kind of fella!

## Maudlin Sentimentality

Mornin' Sergeant Major
How do to you
There's a bugler outside playin' a distant tune
I never thought about all the robins, blackbirds, starlings chattering away
But there you go; the bugler plays his one and only tune

Only it's half past four and I'm tryin' to get some kip
What with all the other things to dream about
It don't half make you twitch
Oh cor blimey, there he goes again
Blowin' on his horn all before the cockerill's dawn
Oh I cannot believe it
There goes another dream
All the way to the courtyard for a marching up and down
All I ever wanted was me bed and the eider down

Can you ask him to come back only it's ruining my glance
While I'm up there in la-la-land floating among the clouds
Seeing girls with their frilly frocks on all jiving to and fro
Until the bully comes along and tore out the bleedin' song!
Can you stop him Sarg I really must insist
So that we can all have a lay in
And maybe we can all get a bit o' kip!

## Stand Alone

Both legs and I
Would like to say: "Thank You!"
For the way you've been.
He has made us see
The glory, the power from deep within
Now how can I?
Get over this momentous act?
Precariously moving through all the facts.
Will I get out of here?
Should I dis-agree?
Won't you look at this now
I've grazed both my knees
Shout it out loud; "for heaven's PEACE!"
Come here, tell me; "I'm not blue in the face!"
Gods must have been crazy
Leaving without a trace
Spent lover
Some dear
Mem-mema mentor
My fff-fears

All that you're asking?
Why then come over here!
We can help each other
There ain't no better way
Least path of resistance
No sense of debate
With answers all here
Let's go - you relate!

## You want to know where I met my wife.

I met my wife at Debenhams. Yes, she worked there from nine to five and bit later on a Friday night. She worked in the lingerie department with a couple of other birds who were pole-dancing specials. Oh you mean, at the local strip joint?

Well, I met mine in Katmandu! She was halfway up a mountain range looking for a bracelet she had dropped whilst riding her bike. She was 16 at the time. I recall meeting her like it was yesterday and with great detail as well. Her bike was the most amazing thing I had ever seen; red in colour with 26" wheels and all. I mean, do you ever see bikes like that these days? The saddle was from Granger Ranger Outfit Co. You know the Outdoor Adventure outlet down on Wardour Street, next to the 'Tin Of Flies & Box of Frogs' store. Well, its number 12 if you really must know.

Anyway, I remember seeing her ride this bike with such apparent ease that I just had to leap out and stop her. The silly sod almost ran me over!

I told her not to get *upset*, as I wasn't hurt or *anything*. I mean, I just wanted to meet her.
I took an instant liking to her posh front lights. Boy! Have you ever seen those systems that charge each and every time you ride the bike? I mean, it's a revolutionary system for each and every step. It's super cool! Though can't find them here. You have to go out there and order them. Hey, perhaps you can find them on the iNet? But, I'm not so sure. It's better to be there and order them man-to-man…or man-o-man if you know what I mean.

Her name is Sally. She was staying at the home hut some five miles away with a couple of burpers and was looking for a bracelet that had fallen off when she was doing some wheelies. This bike is really amazing! I just had to get a closer look at her if I thought that I was ever going to get a ride on it!
Being the charming person I be, I took her out on the dirt track of an afternoon and asked her, very politely, if I could ride her bike. Geez, I had never been too embarrassed in all my life. I mean, it's not everyday you get to see a bike like that, let alone ride one.

So I rode the bike three times 'round the course and then asked her to go to the cinema. This is where we really got upset because there was no parking space left outside and we had to keep our bikes under lock and key. The guy at the cinema said it was all right to park the bikes at the back and we could collect them when the show was over. This was brilliant really! The film was a load of crap! We kept looking at our watches and brushing our hair, smiling at each other wondering if it was time to go back out and just ride our bikes.

Aye mate, we were a couple of likely lads back then – them were the days alright! You want another pint with that chaser?

## Bedroom eyes

She's a slut, she's a whore
She's got everything and more
But she gotta live and boy how she lives

She's a slut, she's a tart
She'll beat you all 'cos she's smart
Don't ye' start out with 'oh you're lyin''
She's the one to start you crying
She knows what you came here for - tryin'

She's a slut, she's a liar
She's the one you temporarily hire
She's got game - you take the blame
Oh but for 'the love of life'
On you she depends
'cos she's gotta live, yes, she gotta live

She's a slut, she's a whore
Boy, she is giving you what for
She's her own man - got all her plans
An early retirement deals in scams
Oh but how she lives
Oh boy how she gives

She's a slut, she's a whore
She'll be honest, she's the bore
Don't you forget it - she will tell it
Far from heaven - it's your call - so hear it!

She's a slut - she's a whore
Boy, you'll wonder what you come here for
Then you pay her and then you pay up
Until you can't get no more
Still, she's got a life to lead
Still, she's got a life to lead

She's got a kid now, where's your baby?
Treat her right - after all she is your lady
She's a whole lot more bedsides - now crawl
She'll break your heart - don't wanna decide
Oh come with me - she's on the other side!
Don't be a fool - just use your tool
Lay it on the sideboard go out with the drool
'cos she's got a life to lead
Yes, she's got a life to lead

Why she does it - no-one knows
It ain't heaven then don't you know
Don't look back - you won't regret it, no!
She's the plan, she's the man
Spreads her wings go get her tan

She's the slut, she's a liar
Boy, she gave you what for, your desires
Her prostitution is no solution
All she wants is to retire
You pay her fees - you get the wires
'cos she's got a life to lead
Yes, she's got a life to lead

She's the rabbit you're the hat
You'll get confused with all of that
She's the feather she's the bee
Boy, will she have you on your knees
When you get up you'll regret it
When you pay up - she'll forget it
You're so down - that's when it hits you
Empty wallet, no te-test-testicles
Buy hey, she's got a life to lead
Yes, she's got a life to lead

All I know is hard to fine
Like the frog a prince and all the wine
She steals your heart then leaves you broke
To protect herself with the words unspoke
She won't do deals without a clash
It's your dick she wants upfront and with the cash
'cos, she's got a life to lead
Yes, she's got a life to lead

Gawd, I wish I knew her pursuits
Into what the heck I am doing here?
Boy, she don't give her credit where credits due
'cos she's got a life to lead
yes, she's got a life to lead

## Piggy Ann Bones.

Piggy Ann Bones came over this afternoon looking for you.
Well I wasn't here was I? Was at the chip-shop looking at some plaice with beady little eyes staring at me when this guys goes; "Hey, do you want chips with that? Or are you just going to stand there waiting for the next castle to come around?"
Well, I wasn't having any of it. What with those 'floozy eyes' and all telling me that fish was definitely off today!
So I packed my senses and left without ordering anything.
Later outside I ran into Pinkie who was sporting a yellow outfit. Oh and how awful he looked in it. It must be really sad to walk around in such colours trying to change your life like that as what he does.

The guys think he's a 'poofta' whilst he himself thinks he's the bees knees. It's in my opinion that girls really wanna a 'hunky guy' than end up with the likes of him. He looks a right old toss pot if you wanna know. Well, you gotta laugh ain't ya? At least he tries. Mind you, I cannot see him hitting on any bird while wearing such attire. I mean, it's just not on it is it? Cor blimey, can you imagine crawling into bed with a canary like that. You grabs hold of his pajamas and he'll peck at your loins for hours not knowing where the bra-straps unlock. It's all so funny. Like I said, I cannot see him getting off with any bird this side of John-'O' Groats. Good luck to him!

Yellow or not, he gotta right to wear just what he likes and if it comes over all so flimsy that that's his problem. We have to look through that.

"You mean, you want me to look through his yellow underpants and see what type of score he has?"
"No! All I am saying is this…it's not the clothes that make a fella. It's his insides, his personality and character that really form the basis of a good person.

Frankly, I find him repulsive and wouldn't go near him. Nor even let him touch me with your hands… eeurgh! It gives me the creeps just thinking about it. Give me a man who knows what he's doing with his hands and knows just where to press the button. Do you think he knows what an orgasm is?

I mean these guys really believe that if they can jump your bones then they get off and leave you halfway up a garden path with a nine-month suspended sentence. 'Ere, it's amazing when you come to think of it. The wants and needs of a woman are basically the same as the guy but he just don't know how to pull it off! I tell you, if ever I meet Joe Bloggs and we decide to get married then that'll be one of the main topics for lots of discussion.  Oooh Err! Quality time! Come what may as the saying goes.

Hey, I have to scoot off now…I bought this dirty magazine and you just put me in the right old mood for tasting it with some time for some solo lo-go and sleazy upshot reading. See ya later!

## Heirs and Graces

Who cares about your heirs and graces?
Who cares about the mess you're making?
Who cares about the dreams you're faking?
Who cares about the no go - do so?
You're picking it up
But you ain't got a clue

You dream about your one life - don't lie
You dream about your big chance - fat chance
You're cleaner than it's one I-O-TA!
You gimme pop I'll give you cream and soda
Don't forget you're picking it up
But you ain't got a clue

Who cares about the scares and places?
Who cares just where the fables faded
Mysteries and you're all escapists
Pull the tow and the next your rabid
You follow me and you might escape it
Through the wilds and winds don't fake it!
You show a smile and you just might make it
Don't forget you're picking it up
But you ain't got a clue!

## Slightly large Joe

Concealed under the placement conjecent to a Cathedral column, came a questionable figure of minute proportion. Under which the following scenario is set;
“Are you here to pick me up?” enquires she.
Not wanting to prolong the little ladies patience with my reply, I ask; “well, how far do you want to go?”
Knowing full well the intricacies of self-worth and of the giggling meanderings lifted slightly toward perhaps leaning on a soft porno tint with hoity-toity ramblings buried beneath therein.
“Well”, I reply quite swiftly; “Yes, indeed I am!”
“Oh that’s great”, says she. “my feet are killing me!”

## Horses for courses

Mummy you look so different today
Are you tired? Are you ill?
Must you take another pill?
Oh daddy please no - don't do that again!
You upset the li'l uns
By playing with that thing!

Why don't you?
Why don't you mind your own business?
And go back to your bed!
Mummy isn't feeling good
I'll make it right
Is that understood?
Oh daddy please no – don't do that again
You upset the li'l uns
Playing with that thing!

Dear God, you must help me Daddy isn't bright.
He's eaten all the furry bits, he's rubbing something on her tits
And I don't understand
Please please please
Give me strength to know the truth
He's making mummy so very ill
Hitting her with his stick

Jesus Christ! He calls out, just as I appear
My mummy's red, I think she's dead
Now I think am in for it
All because of his little stick!

Mummy, mummy what is it?
I'm alright my poppet
Don't you worry none
Daddy's gone to wash up
It was only a bit of fun

Dear God, thank you for this day
As I learned another lesson
I learned to stay away
Mummy's fine
Daddy's fine
End of a perfect day?

## Mammie's Kissing

I want my mammie
I want my daddy
I want Santa to be near me
I don't want bottles
I don't want wash
I don't want any of that
Hobble-bosh

Mammies kissin"
Daddies gone
Maybe down the pub
Or maybe he went fishin'
I want my mammie
Pity-poo, beeh-hoo
I want my mammie
Can't you see?

Santa's comin'
Lots of treats
Better clear the floor now
Why earth beneath my feet
Mammies kissin'
Daddy's gone
Maybe down the pub
Or maybe he went fishin'
I want a sweety
In my mouth
Gosh this is such a lotta lolly
I want my mammie
Pity-poo, beeh-hoo
I want my mammie
Can't you see?

Santa's comin'
Down the fire
Better turn it off mammie
Before the smoke expires
Mammie's kissin'
Daddy's gone
Maybe down the pub
Or maybe he went fishin'

## To the right said Fred?

Gangrene's the teenager
Caught up in ruthless rights
Circumcision sizeable
Too small to make a difference
No severance pays
No attorney wails
Yet truth is kept away
It's hidden in the rooftops
Underneath bright lights

To the right said Fred
To the right said Fred
You didn't come together
So it hurts your head!

Auntie May said one day
Beareth fruits that we all plant
My goodness gracious! What a tease!
Them daisies dropped in peas!

To the right said Fred
To the right said Fred
You didn't come together
And it hurts your head!

## Cheeky!

Remembering a hand held high
With a wallop to my face
You cheeky li'l bugger
Now go some other place!

Releases of emocity
Those rages unexplained
Gloating on an airwave
Freed of awful pain
I once saw black
Now I see light
Those darker times of helpless plight

Burdened by a boundary
Escapes my precious clue
The hand held high
I touch the sky
Not realizing its truth

Comfort by a word
Whispered in my ear
At night I criticize it
Though let it go – here and now
Upset I do give in
It wears me thin
Here comes the dream
Just let me in!

Awakened by the sounds of voice
A sound that is so real
In out up or down
When will I get the truth
For all we know there is no truth
Except to you you are on your own!

## Resonating Moments

To know is to LOVE
To LOVE is to know
The meaning of LOVE
Can be exceedingly slow!

Tranquility derives from peaceful belongings
Of peaceful thought with no interpretations or false acumen
Taken in doses can be quite good for your health

Stubbornness derives from having to do something you do not want to do
Ignorance derives from being stubborn
Negligence is therefore stubborn
Forgetting that "it" is there; is only human
Humans have feelings – largely built around a character and personality

Implications are not withstanding
Ideals for better or for worse
Combinations are in many folds
The key to life is LOVE
You find LOVE you get life!
Improvisation is a solemn note, a decree of wanting pure harmony
A wish is not a command
It is a longing for yet on demand!

## Crickey!

Crickey they once told me
Underneath the stars
My Latin spent
I underwent
Translations all in awe

Inspiring time
Creating mine
Though costly, do adore
Caring moments, evermore
Two saviors who gave it all

Leaving me, though teasing me
There's no comfort in a joy
One birdie sings
A waterfall
The dog bite held within

Old Plato, oh Pluto!
Aris-tottle
De-march the March hare
Apollo appalling
A mere change in crawling
Forgiven Saint Stevens
He won't make it even
Four different ways
Of skinning a cat!

## Sadness

Let's cut this sadness its bringing me down
Let's look up this as breaking new ground
If it's the freedom then lets get close to it
If it's the madness then, yeah I am close to it

I don't want the reasons you challenging me
I'm not that evil – something's bothering me
I suspected a truth and then the lies
Though came close to, what a surprise!

Speak for a moment
The glory divines
Forever holy
Our hearts are entwined

Cannot release nor break free as I wanted
There's the matter that puts is aside
It is oh so cheaply well under-rated
For not only beauty
The calls are un-dated

My wants my needs
My purple hearts decease
Red Cross a Union Jack
Wonder why they want it back
I love my country, deep rooted inside
I hate it at home, can't hold this being alone
Needing a comfort of a lovely home
Need people that share life not some thunder dome

My wants my needs
My purple hearts decease
Red Cross a Union Jack
When, when's it all coming back?

## Sunday Musings Ye Olde England

"Of course I never knew the assailant," your honor "I happened to step into the bathroom of a morning and saw her.
And that's the naked truth me honor. Never touched her.
If me eyes were not averted I may have succumbed my ability to flounder - but flounder I did not.
Far from it my Lord - far from it. I was I was all about Ooo five feet away at least - she had lovely - ooh yes, what the eye can see though mustn't tell - she had these enormous.. well to do, you could say towels but I think they were blankets. They were hanging over the bathtub."
I ran up a cold sweat, and that's when she grabbed me!
"Hurry," she said "I want you".

Well 'efore I knew it she was on me loins and doin' the fandango like some crazy woman possessed me Lord.
When she'd done, she spat on me and said, "get out - I don't like strangers!"
And so, I went on me merry way - never to see her again.

Only nine-months later did I hear of a royal wedding and that was when I noticed her again.

She was leanin' up against the railin's waving a very small but quite colourful flag. I caught her eye. She smiled and walked over towards me. I adjusted my wears and tipped and doffed my hat in order to greet her; "G'day ma'am. Lovely to see you - nice clothes you have on -".

Whereby she battered her eyelids not making any sound and made gestures to make me to follow her - which I did - ooh I did your honor.

I followed her right up to the churchyard and it was in the back that she grabbed hold of me once again and before I could say, 'here hold onto this' she was at it again. This time with much more fervour!

But, I couldn't go much longer and gave in to her demands and those wicked ways and so I gave her one of my barleycorn dewdrops - they are from Mason's Avenue, 2/5d a packet - they really are so sweet and value for your money too.

And when she started sucking on it - it was ecstatic Me Lord.
Now she wants to get married and have children who run a sweetshop but the funny thing is your honor - is I'm already married and got a lotta sweets..

## I am in New York

I am in New York and in New York
It's the place that I am crowned in
Though I don't know how and I don't know why
The state am in am frowning
Yet, I don't know how to loose it!

Betty Grable dared upon Times Square
Market stalls and subway fares
Though I don't know why
I wear this frown
And I don't know how to loose it!

Guess am in too deep
Where the apple's a peach
But I don't know how to prove it
Betty Grable gasped
'Such a daunting task
You got to loose yourself then loose it
Now you're much too young
Go and have some fun
Boy you got to go just groove it!"

Now it treats me good like I knew it would
Though think it was unheard of
Now I pay my dues
As I stripped my blues
For the shoes all done they bored me

Packed a bag then launched a rag
To be sure one that I am pleased with
It can't be wrong
So when I sing this song
All for the laughs I get its pleasing
It ain't so daft when I see that craft
With an angel hanging from it

The most amazing sound
As I hit the ground
It's the one that I am drowned in
"in New York – there  I make no sound
'cos the sound there is so confusing"

## Sausage Sandwich

There ain't nothing like a sausage in a sandwich
There ain't nothing like a sausage in your mouth
You might as well as wonder
It gives and takes your hunger
So you better eat one now and everyday

There ain't nothing like a sausage in a sandwich
There ain't nothing like a sausage in your mouth
Some find it cool and horny
The taste of brine and boar meat
A li'l mustard on the top
Four starters it's the crop
So you better eat one now and everyday

There ain't nothing like a bread roll in the morning
There ain't nothing like a good role late at night
Oh for sure those southern comforts
Look them up they're evening standards
Drop your guard; well on your knees
Give in to the chipolatas
Short on onions ketchup mustard
Sure takes a lot to get to please
There ain't nothing like a sausage in a sandwich
There ain't nothing like a sausage in your mouth!

## Bernie the Bolt

In, out shake it all about
Up, down wiggle it a bit
Right, left attention all
East, west your paw knows best

From this once can decide
Circles, squares okay, alright
Log ins sides all great
Equal to the number
On a steak I plate

Totally the circumference round
Appealing attire watches til
The sun goes down
Moon crescent on a full day bright
Nothing but contradiction
Pending ever visual light

Hubble hobble
The clear sky new
Wobbling about like
There's no rescue
Can u see it?

Oh he's clever ain't he Tom
Uncle George so full of satire
The auntie Mabel do
In, out shake it all about
Wiggle it a bit
Left right squeeze in tight
Hold yer horses
Not that tight!

## Mount conscience

Music captured me when I was so small
Thirteen years of hunger, man I was so tall!
With thoughts of ever after love
Streams of angels from above
To travel far on wings of doves
Come shining through the God of Love
A sequence

Once I took an overdose in drinking
Could barely live a life worth living
Everything I so adored
Man, woman, the tears next door
In search of alibi's to rid my conscience held on high, neatly
Though now I'm just a whim, the scorned out kid, the bum, a pimp!
Anything a man can ever dream of
Now all I seek are alibi's to rid my conscience held on high, politely

Late last year was ever dreamy, oh yes indeedy
I met this girl then I don't know
Her kisses were as white as snow
I really miss her
Oh for the comforts
Thoughts of neither here nor there
Taken drink then retire in awe not despair
The truth is that I cannot take it
All in all I just can't fake it
So what am I supposed to know?
The girl ran off, oh don't you know
I'm leaving
Why just last week I bought my ticket
Am off to Lords without a wicket
Sounds easy listening
Where is one supposed to go?
You work it out, 'cos I don't know
I'm lost!

## The dessert naked one

One day I was happy as can be when all of a sudden I got one of the most horrific headaches of all, namely, the confrontation with a manipulator. You know that 'being' that can do no wrong? That if you don't believe in it, will set things up so that in fact you are still wrong.

Now I generally talk myself through a lot of situations before-hand and weight up the pro's and cons in balance and therefore ask myself, "why has life come to this? What did I do to deserve this and such a life? Why is everyone so sex-mad, power driven, money crazed and just downright deceitful? What on earth have I done?"

The conversation piece with myself goes something like this; "Oh I hate it. This life is getting me down grinding and grinding until there is no more. Got no time nor energy for this nor that. Those nagging questions that are so simple that I have to think, re-think and re-do everything over and over again – it is very tiring boring and tedious".

While a voice says; "Why don't you turn to God and to Jesus?"
I say; "I have spent enough time learning the good the bad ways. I am now trying to live, to survive yet am failing miserably by being manipulated. It's everywhere I go. Do I look like a robber or a thief? Maybe a mugger, a rapist, a terrorist, a suicide bomber, an assassin, perhaps I might be the forgerer too?"
He says; "No, though you do look like the devil."

I said; "What? I'm certainly not a devil. You can get that out of your head right now mate!"

"Oh?" says he; "then prove it! Take a look around you. What kind of life you are leading right now? Look at, in particular at the life that you had and the one you still cling on to?"

"Well, if you put it like that", says I; "I do live in a bit of a bad state – I'll clean it up later. People, in my view are entitled to some privacy far away from such prying eyes. So yes, okay okay then I do live in Hell."
"Well there you go" says he; "you are living proof of the devil. You are your own worst enemy. Is there anything else you need?"

My thinking at this time causes yet another very bad surge in my ongoing headache pain. In fact I don't want to be discussing such matters of religion whether they are deemed true or not.

It was at this time that I was barred from speaking directly to anyone and have since been in ex-communication with voices being bounced off of a wall. Direct contact has been severed for I had breached the line of command and of authority whereby a zillion other charges were suddenly trumped up against me! It's a form of capitol punishment and I am held up serving out its sentence.

By visiting my local church one day I was led out the front door quite sternly by the arm of the priest who was telling me that it was closing time and I would have to come back some other day.

Then shortly after upon making a visit to a local café for a cup of coffee was heard as being 'the drunken skunk of the town' and 'was not allowed to park his butt in here'. Phew, I apparently smelled too much. Hands being waved before faces and other such bodily gestures.

Followed by, when I was strolling around the local park heard clear voices of; 'there he is again, he's still looking for it. hihi he won't find it here..that stupid man…what an idiot!'

Other commentary in bits and pieces out there went like this; "he's only got a couple more years to live anyway" and "all of a sudden he don't like Chinese food."
This all to me is negativity speaking street-talk with gross overtones in mind-manipulation.
For it is not me speaking audibly nor uttering these words. Those thoughts have never entered my head!

Though it is clearly what I hear!

Ah, but it's wrong to speak bad of thy neighbour, parents, elders, peers and you should know that. Of course I know that and I do understand the implications fully.

Yet, again the joker, that manipulator, pops his ugly head up stating; "you are doing it all wrong."

To me personally, de-meaning an awful state of 'mind over matter' I shout; "You are the manipulator and not I!".

Having said that, very bad things begin to happen.
My headache takes another turn for the worse.

I don't believe words that are not spoken to me directly.
I trust no one - everyone seems to have the very same sick frame of mind!

I go off on my own in search of peace and quite far away from such dealings.
Some call it 'soul-searching'. No! It isn't that!? I just need to get away from this hurtful painful reminder that I am actually being called a devil and for being made out so that I would appear so. It's a gross injustice on my person and I find it most irregular.

Remember, the manipulator goes to great lengths to prove his/her point.

In the public eye and in public opinion they are regarded and respected as the foremost and upright of all human beings. Everyone listens to them.

Therefore they can turn it about and set it out just as they like?
They can have their field day after all and capture the cliché perfectly 'they can have their cake and eat it too!"
They will manipulate you into forms of submission and into a state where you have to own up, wise up and blurt it all out like the big crybaby that you are. But, big but, as to what you have done wrong is mind-boggling to say the least – no one will ever tell you - it is 'a mind' at work.

Meanwhile, they make the sale where spices and prices go up and up and then they go down. Trillions are knocked off. Accidents will happen they say – yet all the while this meandering body hangs around pounding death into your head killing thousands in reality in the process.

Listen I spake, "I respect your point of view. Though I am no devil and I am no God either.
Though, what I do see is a manipulator and it has to stop! I don't want to be the one to change the spots on a leopard but I do see a cheater! I don't like them and I don't like you – go away!"

So it's curtains after all.
The manipulator stands where he has always stood and that is; in the way! And by the way is just a stones throw away. I find it abusive the ways and means of getting a submission for whatever reason that may be.
The pressures coming from all sides and walks of life in whatever form that may be.

I speak some more; 'Why, they could make the mute talk and sell sand to the Arabs and those that actually live on the darn stuff!"

Like the best kids at play, some are very polite and some are better seen and not heard. Some regard it as a feat and they have to win it. Others feel that whatever they do isn't going to help the dire situation. All the while the weaker and weaker body keeps falling to the wayside being stepped on, trodden on and made out as the biggest enemy the world has ever seen on God's Earth! Quackers by jove! Its kosha crap!

Let me state this fact and for the record; what has been taught you, was taught me also, as it was stated; "let no man pull us under, together we will stand strong" and was signed by God hisself. (X)

However, there are also false Gods and seeing them is left down to the eyes of the bee holder. You get stung each and every time whether you wanted to be or not.

Understanding this statement I stayed here trying to prove myself of some worth and ended up in the gutter, very angry, very bitter, very cold and also very dead!

One day I was laying turning in my grave and there appeared once more a figure stating that I should have listened to what he had to say. Yeah right!

By this time my ears had fallen off and were eaten by the worms, snails, grubs, maggots and spiders. I thought to myself it's a pity he didn't have a sense of humour, I could have told him his flies were open!

You see, even in my grave there are manipulators!

Help?!

## Ching Chong

Ching Chong lives in China on a boat near potpourri
He lives a life so gorgeous he changed it suddenly

His father was Confucius was clever with it too
When mother came to join them she didn't quite pull through

Now he's out there on his own sailing all round Beijing
Has lots of fun, his tank top on and boy can he still sing!
Yade ho ya de he ...
Yade de hey ho ...

Su Lin came to see him and looked him straight in the eye
Though he answered not just gave a nod with some turkey and stir-fry
Let's go
Yade ho ya de he ...
Yade de hey ho ...

Forget not when you see him
His numbers' forty-two
With a gift wrap on
The curtains drawn
With steaming prawns!
Yade ho ya de he ...
Yade de hey do ...

## Dream like you

I clamber up the hillside
Feel the wind push me aside to somewhere
God knows where

The feeling in my legs grows cold
I'm ageless as time has told
(well you should have known better
'cos you've just been rolled).
Down - down - down - go down - so slow

Feel the pain beneath my feet
Rise up as I kill the heat
I said I will not be beat!
No I will not be beat!

Why is it that life seems to take so long
Especially when you've been let down?
Then some girls gets a hold onto
Spreads your wings then fly onto...

Dreams like these seem such a sacrifice
Death seems twice as nice
Hung and dry are these tears that I cry
Those beautiful times all gone and run away.

Dreams like you will never come true
If I don't get up and try
Maybe I can run, maybe I can hide
Lady there ain't no telling
Where I can hitch a ride.

I hear them saying that you're a basket case
Come over here and think you own the place
Strife, brittle, battle wires what a corny desire
Get your own money and don't you play with fire
Grow up little boy, there's a new world waiting for you
All you gotta do is stand up and take what's before you

I wanna be around you
Fill your heart astound you
Build your hopes on soft ground
Share the love, spinning around.

## The Sunflowers

The flowers are exceptionally cold this season
The rain leaves much to be desired
Mr. & Mrs Sunflower are expecting seedlings.
Good old sounds of pitter-patter on the mud;
"Delve deep little ones - for the earth is rich and good".

Standing two meters tall
Where did I leave me shovel?
Grannies dead and buried,
Grandad he went to war.
Yes, in our house, like a bees -nest
There's honeydew; it feeds us

Gosh, I am so very tired
I need to take a rest
Lying here - just catch my breath
Let Mother Nature do the rest

R.I.P as they will say
One day upon my grave
Lest we pray; behold, my children laugh
And rise again shall I,
Through the wonders of an age old myth
Of time and evolution - life!

Now praise the Lord my soul to give
And keep me warm inside
A glow of peace in troubled times
My memories, a myth
God Bless You!

## Blood Money

Third watch
Men threaten threads of cotton
Ladies linger longer looming lust
Combined fortitude
Straighten up a costume (jacket).

Blood money brothers: Quiver and Salinko.
Penetrating wisdom leaves nothing for chance
Losses considered
Far outweigh the combined harvest that is a twist.

Underneath the hopes, the melancholics drivel
Sometimes for all eternity
Sometimes not a quibble.

Two hundred years still under repression
Am always in denial - I learn to say 'NO'
One day or another
What does it matter?

Sad, sadder and under disgrace
Nothing else matters
Whatever your choice
It is written in your face.

## Not I

I liked the way you told me
I wondered: 'is that true?'
For all the time that I have known
Were lies devoid of truth?

I didn't like the look-a-like
So I watched it, from the side
Amazing grace avoided place
The secrets kept not one divide

Challenges not fought within
Though priceless, priced again
The sculptures sought was understood
My woolied feathered friend..
And then he went and said: 'Not I!'

## Off The Cuff

Pink think ice on a full score board
Matters of construction unto matter borne
Pretty is a colour, what you get is juice
Trouble meaning manners and there is no excuse

Opperandi Mandy
Gilbert Baggins tools
Humbug to another
Is this getting through?

Then suddenly, realise
Uh oh junk fed food on a bed of nails
Kumuaro Sara
Tahiti whacko Joe
Coming round the corner
Just to see my show
Deliberertly!

Opperandi Mandy
Gilbert Baggins tools
Humbug to another
Is this getting through?

Thin blue rope on a toe skin tight
Wazzamattabuddy ain't this right?
Jumble up a romance, no loving there at first
Hahahaha blink - well - I thought you might!

Opperando Mandy
Gilbert Baggins tools
Humbug to another
Is this getting through?

## I'm buggered if I know

Grandad handed me a medal, he'd won it in the war
He told me of the time he spent and how it took his all.
He said: 'been wounded in the back by a Jerry they called John
In fact it was a lady dressed up in a uniform.
At night I'd fall asleep with nothing but bread crumbs and some water.
But at night is when the rabbits hunt, as I dreamt of the Generals daughter.

Suddenly, there's a white light all flashes from behind
The guns ablaze the noise pace for tears with no dry eyes
I quickly turned towards it, ducking as you do
When a bayonet caught me by surprise, oh by golly was it cruel!
A painful cry on one so high, ecstatic some might say
Then as I looked around - there was no sound
So I slept the whole darn day!

Guilt as someone called it, evasive, jaded and obtuse
Yet, what you got to win when you got nothing left to loose?
Jolly me oh golly be, praise the Lord for having me
Now I know what's become of me, I'd left it all behind.

Though some might say, "it's Jerry's day" I doubt it all the same
Sitting here besides you, I'm very grateful in a way
My life's been spared; I saved the day by breathing in fresh air.
So, whenever there's a war on, think of this medal do.
Put it down your Y-fronts for safe keeping and boy will it look cool.
Those horny little buggers though daft as it may seem
Think of all the medals won my son and a bum that won't be creamed!"

Thank you and goodnight!

## Ode to the life less living

Ode to the wondrous clouds out there
All puffy and white without any care
Ode to the blooms
Ode to the crispy shallow waters proud
Ode to the wild nights
Ode to the delights
Ode to the essence of all our lives

Ode to the dream Gods and those upon high
Ode to the everlasting crystal skies
Ode for the moments all pure and simple
An ode to the Goddess of temptations triple

Under the warm lights those stars at a distance
Ode to the wonders of all mankind
Prefab the cup-cakes, donuts upon rye
Ground down coffee and hazelnuts where walls were mind
Ode, Ode ode, Ode-eur!

Ode to dominion fall soft as a feather
Darkest the hour, cor blimey the weather!
Wonder the seamstress all frilly and frocks
Ode to manhood well into his socks

Ode for the rubble a place shattered and torn
Ode to the one who pulled out a thorn
Ode for the meager grey and the mire
Ode for the tigers the lions and some ghastly fires

Ode to the man who gets things done
Who you call me so I ain't no bum
Ode to the love's and will you marry me
Will you make me happy
Will you help me to see
With an ode to the mongers, those beggars them pawners
Ode to the essentials in your kinder old ways.

## Chinese?

Did you get the Chinese?
I did not get the Chinese.
Have you seen those hieroglyphics?
They sure do look terrific

One birdie here and a kitten over there
The water flows and some gold bits over here

The pinnacles of fortune
Mummy knew it too
But did she utter; not a word
The pyramids a clue

Somehow chocolate destroys it
Darth Vader foxes too
It's snowing here
With hustlers there
I wonder what they gotta prove

It's business as usual
Down the dust pipe too
Forging anthems
There's a bantam
Crickey! Clucking poo!

## Feather Like

Seasons come as durex go
You wonder where the time does go
We age and age as we gather pace
A look at life and the human race

Sometimes we're jolly
Sometimes we're folly
Most of all we're on life's trolley
Crawling about making those sounds
And calling out when it all comes out

Trouble in need is trouble indeed
A friend you once had now squalled seed

Snow brushes on an evening gown
Feather like - endearing - twilight

Well excuse me for now fitting in
I've got a life to live and it's wearing me thin!

## The Indian Times

Three scalps and a jurisdiction
The Indian Times and a bull ring too strong
Feathered cap in an Ascot dress
Worn out boots in an army chest

Seargent Major, Corporal Healer
Sir Edward Heath and the East Cheam drearies
Mantovani to Mussolini
General De Gaulle and the Cold Stream bladders
Wormwood Scrubs and the White Washed willies

Turner Boots with a cat called coat
Budgerigar on the toadstool platter
Under the bridge it is mind over matter

Sodom and tomorrow
The day they gotta swallow
The partin' of waves
Where Timothy say;
Memphis! Nigeria!
All retained here for Her Majesties Pleasure!

## Adamo

September won't wait another second
For a freedom flight, one for the record
Sitting in the rold call seat
Turn up the noise - turn up the heat
God say; "you crazy", I want that beat

Tied down like a wounded rabbit
Curled up in a ball feeling savaged
Don't wanna be a hero
Don't wanna scream no more
Though giving up my ticket
Gonna cost me more

Don't you tantalise me
Or even re-arrange me
I need nobody of can't you see
It's here where it all happens
Underneath the lights
Forever in a debt and you don't think twice

So they get a little stronger
Push a little harder
But the truth is getting to me
I can breathe no longer
Suddenly it's evil - sitting in the clouds
Oh how hard the trigger when it makes no sound
Fly by - fly by - fly by - bye - bye!
No longer is it here - fighting with a devil
He got no breath though he smells like gravel

## Woe's Life (Spearhead)

I am so naturally melancholy looking
Nothing much creative about me

Why, even sordid details can abate it
If you ever know how much the hunger
No palpitation factors can release

Supportive gestures never under written
Fourth protocol to boot and remittance
Where an angel sings a lullaby (heavenly)
God grants his grace
No fear of man
This is the place...

Peacefully pictured in kaleidoscope
Carrousels, a twinkle in the corner of an eye

Transcendental energy - mental enemy
Don't fight it - delight it!
Where angels sing their lullaby (heavenly)
God grants his grace
No fear of man
This is the place...

## Old Time Lemons

You remember Jayne out of L.A
Flew a little closer to the sun?
You remember Lorna with her buns?
Her rolls were mighty plenty
But for those she charged you twenty
I never knew a moment from a while.

You remember Joe he took your ego
Tossed it in the air - created fun?
You remember Peter - whose sight has gotten weaker
As we elevate the corner stones of life and
I never knew a moment from a while.

Can you remember Wailings back in Orleans?
Or Jeffersons; the Jones' of Alderney?
You recall the anger - look at my best friend
You kicked him into to touch without a care
Now all he has is breathin'
With a gorgeous chick to feed him and
I never knew a moment from a while.

You recall the time we had in Hampstead?
Wild horses ran then blew away our chances
Those zebra's were conceited
Just like the boys unseated!
Boy, I haven't had so much fun for a while
But you know
I never knew a moment from a while.

## No Principles

Well I ain't no scapegoat
Nor a chicken on remote
I do have principles
Though I don't need to gloat

Smile here - smile there
Nothing seems to work
Am in bad luck Dave
It's driving me berserk

Nothing going my way
Outward bound
In an awkward town

It don't do me justice
Living on a cloud
So what do you do about it?
The overbearing truth?

Life is such,
Life is such,
Life is such

I can't do owt about it
Overbearing youth
Why don't we just call it
Why don't we just call it
A truce!

## Planetary Escapism

Venus, watch it
Vino... it goes
I know
I know
IO.

Major Callista, Pheobe
Don't you want it; maybe?
Suddenly the stranger
Takes a tumble
Photographed in colour
What a blunder

Secret sequence oily
Flexes muscles
Dribble in and out
It's all the go

Wonder how far the eye goes
Listen while I tune in on you

## Arty Orchard

On every branch a hundred leaves
Topped by fruits and tasty treats

An apple here and an apple there
It doesn't mean much when they grow everywhere

Some say its madness
More signs of depression
Though relaxing to some
When born under discussion.

Funny how it is
A squirrel hangs there
Probing around for the fruits
And grubs to be found
His bushy old tail made for a cover of sorts
Maybe it keeps him warm
Or then maybe not.

## Sorry

I'm sorry for keeping you awake at night
Though tears and shame make a river, right?

Sudden reminders
Proposals
Some kind
Haunting return to places divine
A short in the dark
A full heart attack

Blatant reminders all shoals and a clam
Point forty-five, rubber Johnny the Benz

Pulling it down
The white water rapids
Come hell or high water

Beacon forlorn and what will you wear
Icicle tops you're now stuck in a rut
Silver lit candles
May burn ever true...

## Geez Us Told 'Em

Forever hungered by the gods on the walls
You keep away 'cos you want it all
I feel unsafe when you are not around
When you are here its a friendly cloud

Feel like the fool who's learning to drive
You got some money honey, I need to buy?
Way down West Coast Saturday night
They're yelling and screaming oh what a sight

Pull up a seater you gotta be mine
Some girls just hose pipe
Drainpipe - mainline

Well you sure look good
Real fine to me
Took you a long time
To get what I mean

Geez us told 'em
Go feather your stock
Pick up a mattress
Don't batter your flocks

Well I dunno mate, sure sounds great
Hanging around here, like I gotta wait
You came here fishing got caught in the heat
I was just down there thinking water under my feet.

## Homestead Town (incomplete)

I miss the football park
I miss the trains that pass
Oh for the Corbett Arms an' darts

Twin spirits on your knees
Last orders if you please
From over and under the worlds gone asunder

Clash - bang - wallop pretty pictures please
Oh for the climbs that I had made
Over the hills and far away

Hear the echoes if you will
Burrowing skylines what a thrill
Saint Stephens's dreary mire
Over Gregorian models the funeral pyres

Downtown to lay it to rest
For a fruitcake in some nest
Got the magic
Beaming smile
Who can run a whole eight-mile

Green green grass and follow in it
Watch it chums you wallow in it
Cutching up and huddled tight
Guess I could camp out here every night

Tweet tweet here
Little birdy there
Upon the quarry and the waterfall
A Dymbeth fairy are you gonna ball?
Do I have to push you you puny li'l punk

## Clock

Look at the clock - it's ticking
Look at the clock - time's running out
Look at the clock - it knows how
Look at the clock - it's showing how
Look at the clock - it's bowing out
Look at the clock - times a mystery

You're fading
Mid-life
Battery low
Mis-guided
Depends upon a look to know
The deficit will grow
Whatever comes - will be now
Look at the clock - you made it!

## Trouser call

Too late the trouser call
I shake my legs I don't know it all
Why do I?
Oh why do I?
Feel at all?
Oh why do I feel at all?

Too dry the costume ball
Far away dresses dance y'all
Kissing you I've been there lately
In my dreams't was jolly batey!

Clear skies - the morning's under
Turn away - the flocks a blunder
Crucified for want of nothing
It gets about by delving - helving
Melvin - calling - drawing neatly storing

Pen and paper the masks of favor
Your lips and glossed but none my flavor
Kiss yourself break out the daylights
Tomorrow comes when this feels so right
Oh ooooh walla, walla
Yahoo, walla, walla, walla

Neat the wind - night falls so fast
Block around a pool gets through paths
And you pass it - pass it
You pass it - everyday.

## Circles

These circles in my veins - remains
Across the table a woman stares
Upon a smile where I take flight
The unknown pleasures to gracious heights

Whatever it wants it surely doth take
By thinking it's so I make a mistake
Accidents will always be
Somewhere - someplace - sometimes

God is my shepherd - I shall not want
He maketh me lie down in green pastures

The devil in plain clothes and dresses for free
Up into heaven all high 'n' mightily
What she don't know can't make him go
Pushing and pulling all angles that be
Inward and outboard, the complexity
Drowning you slowly, in no company
She don't know the different
She ain’t learned the ways
She writes in a language that we all mistake
Come what, come not
She's down on your luck
She does everything for you - anything, for a buck!

## Arms to an angel

Slow movement tangible, twisting cubism
Array brightness clever clogs
Heavy head, the junk food lies
Pillow talks no dreams allowed
Under wraps a Berne for crying out loud!

Arms to an angel
These wings unfold
A gift of the moment
Boisterous and bold

Seasons are they calling
Where's the rain, is it falling?
Warm is the color dew
My lover this is crawling

Its business as usual - you let it be
Wind blowing gently
My penitence, my goodness, grief!

## Questioning?

If ever I should loose my faith in you
Forgive me love for I know not what I do
I feel this way because am fooled
Unfortunate circumstances
Keep it apart
Mishaps, delays, troubles, mistakes
All under the hat

Arguably I need it no more
Peace is a hunger and I want more
Don't wanna close where I left off
Need a fresh start - a new trough

You are the angel
Undo my sight
Put me to rest
In the place you like

## History heckled me

Richard the third five men from Mars
Henry the eighth and a one armed guard
Subjectively, preposedly objecting name presumably
Doesn't matter anyhow you can get there by car

Over to the TC-Titan under stars
Overrated characters orderly's and bars
Whatever is 'the comfort zone?'
We market from afar

Sanctimonious acrimony whistles until dawn
Beheaded like that lady back in 1444
Jurisdictions' amiable dunking to adore
Foreign language package deals unto matters scorn

Did it leave a message from the man upstairs?
He's the killer-murderer though too late to ignore
Now I don't know what it is you want
You are getting out of hand, all you do is go on
With you and those sordid little plans
Nothing is ever like this you sure do pull it from a hat
Like capturing a rabbit until a rabbit is zapped!

## Thief of hearts

I picture you
You picture me
You running wild through the emerald isles
Of ether regions of happier times

You swore back then to those who knew
To vow revenge on those so few
Those troubled times you so looked down your nose
Turned up laughing though grieving at a ghost

I wondered then as I wonder now
How ailing ills can foretell your tale
To move around and sway your slave
Of hungry times and those war machines

Those heavenly bodies
Counted on as deals
Though stealing is just a game for you
A thief of hearts and I pictured you

I figured there's something most overlooked
A chance of survival that was understood
Both eating off of the cart-wheels ragings and more
I didn't even know what I came in here for

Thinking who's watching who and who's watching the phone
There's a meal in the oven and my stomach's a moan
I picture you
Yet you pictured me.

## Wilbur

Home just ain't the same without Wilbur
Without Wilbur home ain't just the same
If Wilbur was his name and fishing was his game
Then I dunno a better life than that poor Wilbur

No I cannot speak another word about Wilbur
His soul is gone - but not forgotten
He was the greatest friend I ever had
He sure showed me how to make it last

No I can't say another thing about old Wilbur
Where the Chinese mandarin a drake
Pulled a muscle just eating steak
He kept it all on his bill for on parole
And he never bat an eyelid the poor old soul

No I can't speak another word about Wilbur
He took it like a man when he failed to make his plans
Now all his dreams come true and I know why

Talking of the things I know about old Wilbur
Wilbur was the best friend I ever had
His soul may he rest in peace
Someday life will hear his reach
'Cos we all know the likes about old Wilbur

Some things you should know about old Wilbur
He was out by the old mandrake just sitting there
All he did was turn around - turn around and just respond
Oh but I guess you all know the stories of the pond

Some things you should know about old Wilbur
Wilbur was the best friend I ever had
Some say that he was of pure gold
I'm sure of that but just don't know
Oh boy - but do I still miss old Wilbur
Wilbur was the best friend I ever had

May his soul now rest in peace?
Up in the heavens on release
Come back Wilbur - yeah, we forgive the geese
I'm sure they didn't mean it
Now every time I go out I see Wilbur
Wilbur my best friend I surely miss

## Wayward matters to an end

Well I'd rather be a chicken than a hen
For all of lifes mysteries and then
I wonder what you do especially the youths

The wayward end to the matter
A customary bow to the other
You might not find it proud but someone in the crowd
Knows a way to how - and does it!

They founded prostitution but also destitution
It's the wayward end to the matter
As a customary bow to the other

You might not think it proud but you take it anyhow
Before somebody else takes away your crown
That's it - that's how goodnight for now!

The wayward matters to the end is a customary bow to the other
It might not make you proud but do it anyhow
They like it in the crowd

You read it in the news
They criticize all points of view
But that doesn't make it somehow

Though truth might not be told you got your ticket (let it go) it was sold
To a smaller looking person you thought that was your burden
Until you get to show up it's the same perversion

The wayward matter to the end is a customary bow to the other?
It's not your sexuality proactive that may be
You might not get a kiss you might not feel the bliss
But in due course you'll make it through the list

The wayward matters to an end a customary bow to the other
It might not make you proud but you do it anyhow
You'll feel much better in the end

If a wayward matters in the end it may not matter - it depends
On what you have on your mind
All around you about you all the time
So don't you go get getting all uptight?
If you think it's not alright
It's what the wayward matters to an end!

## Your Thunder

Some people like to watch
Some people like to roll
I just watch them quietly
It makes me very old

Do I listen to your thunder
Do I listen without ears
Do I live a life of luxury
Or do I live with all these fears?

You make me wanna dance
You make me wanna rise
I just lay here quietly
Don't sound so surprised

Though fear maybe your wisdom
A wall to oh so few
I believe in honestly
Something that's new to you

Robbing me a banquet
Filling up my chest
Feeling oh so down again
Goto get myself some rest

## Mish Mash Mosh

Mish Mash Mosh
Mash a large portion of
Smashing
Mash all arts
Got yer Judo, Karate,Taikwondo etcetera

Mischievous behavior
Mashingle, passion for flowers
Mash twat in East side of London
Mash his directed at me

Mish mash mosh
Have a bit of a bosh
Mish mash mosh
Come and have some nosh
Mosh,come on, show us your tosh!

## Sort of Sorts

What kind of mother says you're ugly?
What kind of mother said you made me puke?
What kind of mother says you are deplorable?
Ignorant the sprog that never was

Always in the way –why don't you go out and play
Out of my hair – get out of my hair
I don't want you here, never needed you here
You burden of my life the one that I despise

You'll pay the price for all those finer things ever removed from my life
Get away from me! I don't want you here today
No mollycoddling nor freaky cuddlings for you!

You are just an agitation upon which no one can see
The poison in the ointment that's not so plain to see
Your father the bastard the one I cannot not believe!
He upped your aunt and fucked the sisters too
Played all the people very close to him
All for a bit o' how's yer father oh come fun
Now look what he's done just ups and leaves what a son of a gun!

A life now ruined where no aching gets relief
Forget the you you who have been appeased
I don't want to talk about it I don't want to speak to you
You are nothing in my eyes a missing bern lost out there in a haze
Just pure bastard, no breed, a waste, oh go on get out of my face!

I like the flowers, plants and trees am enthusiastic about hiking
Viewing the sights and all panorama's
Am overly contented with the chores
Some time to reflect her professional life the best
Now should I ever waver then I'll walk it off somehow
Cutting through the nagging the stuff I don't deserve

I like the flowers, just bring me flowers dance me to the end of the show
I want flowers, you bring me flowers orange, whites and violets, bring them now!
And bring me the best!
Oh you're the best! Oh so heaven's blessed look at those!

Goodnight mom, have a good journey

What kind of mother says you're ugly?
What kind of mother says you made her puke?
What kind of mother says you are adorable?
Growing up a kid that never was!

Goodbye you
Goodbye you
Goodbye to you
Farewell, tu jour!

**My thank you for reading list:**

www.ingramcontent.com/pod-product-compliance
Ingram Content Group UK Ltd.
Pitfield, Milton Keynes, MK11 3LW, UK
UKHW061706190726
13853UKWH00008B/2429